Roses
IN CROSS STITCH

Jane Alford

MEREHURST

Published in 1993 by Merehurst Limited
Ferry House, 51-57 Lacy Road, Putney, London SW15 1PR
Text & charts copyright © 1993 Jane Alford
Photography & illustrations copyright © 1993 Merehurst Limited
ISBN 1 85391 063 5
Reprinted 1994, 1995, 1996, 1998

A catalogue record for this book is available from the British Library.

Managing Editor Heather Dewhurst
Edited by Diana Brinton
Designed by Maggie Aldred
Photography by Debbie Patterson
Illustrations by John Hutchinson
Typesetting by BMD Graphics, Hemel Hempstead
Colour separation by Fotographics Limited, UK – Hong Kong
Printed in Hong Kong by Wing King Tong

Merehurst is the leading publisher of craft books and has an excellent range of titles to suit all levels. Please send to the address above for our free catalogue, stating the title of this book.

CONTENTS

INTRODUCTION

Roses, one of the most familiar of our flowers, are represented in just a few of their many forms in this book. Rambling roses around the cottage door, epitomizing a quiet, romantic way of life, are worked in pink french knots in the Rose Cottage picture. The set of three cushions uses bright pink roses and blue and mauve flowers in three different scenarios – a wreath, a large basket and a chequerboard design of baskets and wreaths. Edged with white lace, these cushions bring a breath of summer to your home.

The soft peach and pink shades in the summer roses picture and the peach roses and rosebuds of the pincushion, lavender bag and bookmark contrast vividly with the rich, vibrant shades of the beautiful set of red roses on pristine white table linen and the magenta roses and violas on the placemat and napkin. Either of these would enhance any table setting.

Cross stitch is one of the oldest, and simplest, of all embroidery stitches. With the help of the instructions on this and the following pages, even complete beginners will find that many of these designs are well within their scope. Other projects use a wide range of colours for shaded effects and will challenge the more experienced embroiderers. Whatever your level of skill, you will surely find a project to catch your eye and bring a special touch to your home.

BASIC SKILLS

BEFORE YOU BEGIN

PREPARING THE FABRIC
Even with an average amount of handling, many evenweave fabrics tend to fray at the edges, so it is a good idea to overcast the raw edges, using ordinary sewing thread, before you begin.

THE INSTRUCTIONS
Each project begins with a full list of the materials that you will require. All the designs are worked on fabrics such as Aida or Lugana, produced by Zweigart. The measurements given for the embroidery fabric include a minimum of 5cm (2in) all around, to allow for stretching it in a frame and preparing the edges to prevent them from fraying.

Colour keys for stranded embroidery cottons – DMC, Anchor or Madeira – are given with each chart. It is assumed that you will need to buy one skein of each colour mentioned in a particular key even though you may use less, but where two or more skeins are needed, this information is included in the main list of requirements.

To work from the charts, particularly those where several symbols are used in close proximity, some readers may find it helpful to have the chart enlarged so that the squares and symbols can be seen more easily. Many photocopying services will do this for a minimum charge.

Before you begin to embroider, always mark the centre of the design with two lines of basting stitches, one vertical and one horizontal, running from edge to edge of the fabric, as indicated by the arrows on the charts.

As you stitch, use the centre lines given on the chart and the basting threads on your fabric as reference points for counting the squares and threads to position your design accurately.

WORKING IN A HOOP
A hoop is the most popular frame for use with small areas of embroidery. It consists of two rings, one fitted inside the other; the outer ring usually has an adjustable screw attachment so that it can be tightened to hold the stretched fabric in place.

Hoops are available in several sizes, ranging from 10cm (4in) in diameter to quilting hoops with a diameter of 38cm (15in). Hoops with table stands or floor stands attached are also available.

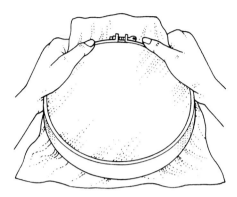

1 To stretch your fabric in a hoop, place the area to be embroidered over the inner ring and press the outer ring over it, with the tension screw released. Tissue paper can be placed between the outer ring and the embroidery, so that the hoop does not mark the fabric. Lay the tissue paper over the fabric when you set it in the hoop, then tear away the central embroidery area.

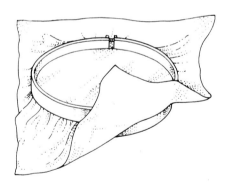

2 Smooth the fabric and, if necessary, straighten the grain before tightening the screw. The fabric should be evenly stretched.

WORKING IN A RECTANGULAR FRAME

Rectangular frames are more suitable for larger pieces of embroidery. They consist of two rollers, with tapes attached, and two flat side pieces, which slot into the rollers and are held in place by pegs or screw attachments. Available in different sizes, either alone or with adjustable table or floor stands, frames are measured by the length of the roller tape, and range in size from 30cm (12in) to 68cm (27in).

As alternatives to a slate frame, canvas stretchers and the backs of old picture frames can be used. Provided there is sufficient extra fabric around the finished size of the embroidery, the edges can be turned under and simply attached with drawing pins (thumb tacks) or staples.

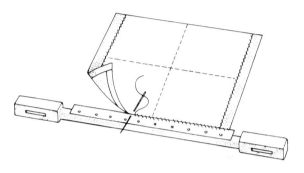

1 To stretch your fabric in a rectangular frame, cut out the fabric, allowing at least an extra 5cm (2in) all around the finished size of the embroidery. Baste a single 12mm (½in) turning on the top and bottom edges and oversew strong tape, 2.5cm (1in) wide, to the other two sides. Mark the centre line both ways with basting stitches. Working from the centre outward and using strong thread, oversew the top and bottom edges to the roller tapes. Fit the side pieces into the slots, and roll any extra fabric on one roller until the fabric is taut.

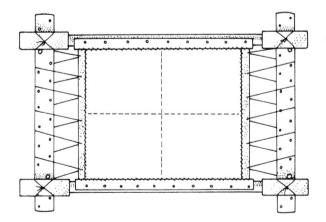

2 Insert the pegs or adjust the screw attachments to secure the frame. Thread a large-eyed needle (chenille needle) with strong thread or fine string and lace both edges, securing the ends around the intersections of the frame. Lace the webbing at 2.5cm (1in) intervals, stretching the fabric evenly.

EXTENDING EMBROIDERY FABRIC

It is easy to extend a piece of embroidery fabric, such as a bookmark, to stretch it in a hoop.

● Fabric oddments of a similar weight can be used. Simply cut four pieces to size (in other words, to the measurement that will fit both the embroidery fabric and your hoop) and baste them to each side of the embroidery fabric before stretching it in the hoop in the usual way.

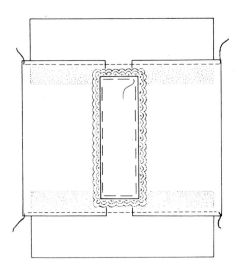

TO MITRE A CORNER

Press a single hem to the wrong side, the same as the measurement given in the instructions. Open the hem out again and fold the corner of the fabric inwards as shown on the diagram. Refold the hem to the wrong side along the pressed line, and slip-stitch in place.

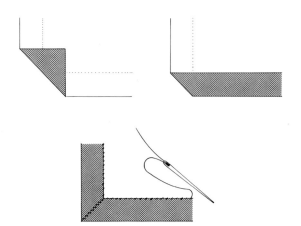

MOUNTING EMBROIDERY

The cardboard should be cut to the size of the finished embroidery, with an extra 6mm (½in) added all round to allow for the recess in the frame.

LIGHTWEIGHT FABRICS

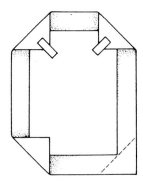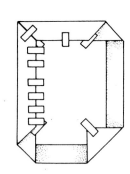

1 Place embroidery face down, with the cardboard centred on top, and basting and pencil lines matching. Begin by folding over the fabric at each corner and securing it with masking tape.

2 Working first on one side and then the other, fold over the fabric on all sides and secure it firmly with pieces of masking tape, placed about 2.5cm (1in) apart. Also neaten the mitred corners with masking tape, pulling the fabric tightly to give a firm, smooth finish.

HEAVIER FABRICS

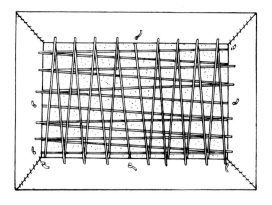

● Lay the embroidery face down, with the cardboard centred on top; fold over the edges of the fabric on opposite sides, making mitred folds at the corners, and lace across, using strong thread. Repeat on the other two sides. Finally, pull up the fabric firmly over the cardboard. Overstitch the mitred corners.

CROSS STITCH

For all cross stitch embroidery, the following two methods of working are used. In each case, neat rows of vertical stitches are produced on the back of the fabric.

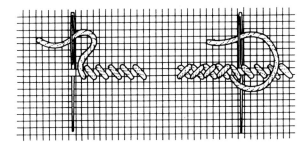

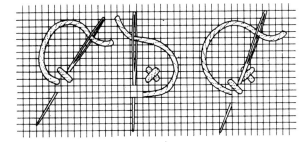

● When stitching large areas, work in horizontal rows. Working from right to left, complete the first row of evenly spaced diagonal stitches over the number of threads specified in the project instructions. Then, working from left to right, repeat the process. Continue in this way, making sure each stitch crosses in the same direction.

● When stitching diagonal lines, work downwards, completing each stitch before moving to the next. When starting a project, always begin to embroider at the centre of the design and work outwards to ensure that the design will be placed centrally on the fabric.

FRENCH KNOTS

This stitch is shown on some of the diagrams by a small dot. Where there are several french knots, the dots have been omitted to avoid confusion. Where this occurs you should refer to the instructions of the project and the colour photograph.

To work a french knot, bring your needle and cotton out slightly to the right of where you want your knot to be. Wind the thread once or twice around the needle, depending on how big you want your knot to be, and insert the needle to the left of the point where you brought it out.

Be careful not to pull too hard or the knot will disappear through the fabric. The instructions state the number of strands of cotton to be used for the french knots.

BACKSTITCH

Backstitch is used in the projects to give emphasis to a particular foldline, an outline or a shadow. The stitches are worked over the same number of threads as the cross stitch, forming continuous straight or diagonal lines.

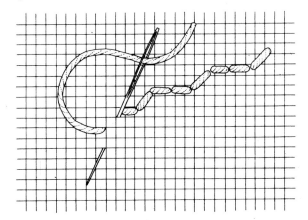

● Make the first stitch from left to right; pass the needle behind the fabric and bring it out one stitch length ahead to the left. Repeat and continue in this way along the line.

ADDING NAMES AND DATES

First of all, on a spare piece of graph paper, draw your names and dates, using the alphabet given for that particular project. Count the number of stitches in the width of each name or date and mark the centre. When you have done this draw the names and dates again, matching the centres with the centre of the sampler.

Rose Corner

Romance is certainly in the air with
this beautiful tablecloth, embroidered
with a ring of red roses and
accompanied by a matching crystal
bowl and silver-framed picture.
This set will brighten up a corner of
the darkest room, and if the bowl is
filled with pot pourri this will provide
a lingering fragrance of summer
to complete the effect.

ROSE CORNER

YOU WILL NEED

For the tablecloth, measuring approximately 1m (39in) square:

90cm (36in) square of white Lugana fabric, with 25 threads to 2.5cm (1in)
Stranded embroidery cotton in the colours given in the panel
3m (3½yds) of gathered lace, 9cm (3½in) wide
No24 tapestry needle

For the bowl lid, with an inset measuring 9cm (3½in) in diameter:

14cm (5½in) square of Zweigart's white 14-count Aida fabric
Stranded embroidery cotton in the colours given in the panel
No24 tapestry needle
Crystal bowl with prepared lid (for suppliers, see page 48)

For the picture, in an oval frame measuring 8cm × 10cm (3in × 4in):

13cm × 15cm (5in × 6in) of Zweigart's white 14-count Aida fabric
Stranded embroidery cotton in the colours given in the panel
No24 tapestry needle
Oval frame (for suppliers, see page 48)

●

THE TABLECLOTH

Prepare the linen and stretch it in a hoop, as explained on page 5. Alternatively, as the even-weave linen is a firmly-woven fabric, it is possible to embroider without a hoop. Following the chart, begin with the central circle, then work outward. Use two strands of embroidery cotton in the needle throughout, and work each stitch over two threads of fabric in each direction.

MAKING UP

Steam press on the wrong side. Make a hem 12mm (½in) deep around the outside of the cloth, mitring the corners (see page 6). Next, measure 24cm (9½in) in each side from each corner and lightly mark the right side of the cloth with a soft pencil, 12mm (½in) in from the edge.

Pin and baste the gathered lace to the tablecloth, positioning the straight edge of the lace 12mm (½in) in from the edge. When you reach the pencil marks, baste the lace across the corner of the cloth, between the two marks. Slipstitch the lace in place.

BOWL LID AND PICTURE

For each, prepare the fabric, basting the central vertical and horizontal lines, and set it in a hoop, as explained on page 5. Use two strands of embroidery cotton in the needle and work over one block of fabric in each direction. Start at the centre of the work and work outward. Steam press the finished work and mount it as explained in the manufacturer's instructions.

Picture ▶

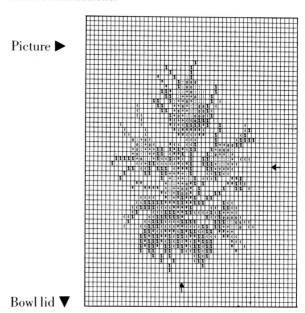

Bowl lid ▼

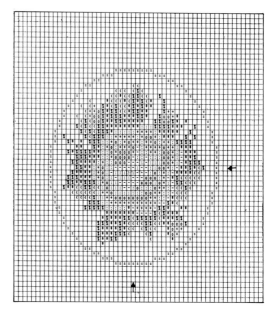

▲
Tablecloth

RED ROSE TABLECLOTH, BOWL AND PICTURE	DMC	ANCHOR	MADEIRA			DMC	ANCHOR	MADEIRA
− Pink	892	28	0413	⟨ Light green		369	213	1309
: Light red	666	46	0210	% Medium green		368	214	1310
+ Medium red	304	42	0511	✚ Dark green		367	216	1312
o Dark red	814	44	0514	= Grey		415	398	1803

Note: One skein of each colour is sufficient for all three designs.

Rose Sampler

A midsummer day's dream is captured in this elegant rose sampler. 'How fair is the rose' showers praise, as rose garlands twine around the sampler. The romanticism of the rose is emphasized by the soft pink, mauve and blue shades of the basket of roses, which creates a charming focal point. Coolness and viridescence wait in the shadows of the olive, sage and lime green shades of the leaves.

ROSE SAMPLER

YOU WILL NEED

For the sampler, with a design area measuring
26.5cm × 31cm (10½in × 12¼in), or 154
stitches by 175 stitches, here in a frame
measuring 42.5cm × 46cm (17in × 18½in):

*36.5cm × 41cm (14½in × 16½in) of Zweigart's
white, 14-count Aida fabric
Stranded embroidery cotton in the colours given
in the panel
No24 tapestry needle
Strong thread, for lacing across the back
Cardboard, for mounting, sufficient to fit in to the
frame recess
Frame of your choice*

●

THE EMBROIDERY

Prepare the fabric and stretch it in a frame as
explained on page 5. Following the chart, start the
embroidery at the centre of the design, using two
strands of embroidery cotton in the needle. Work
each stitch over one block of fabric in each
direction. Make sure that all the top crosses run in
the same direction and each row is worked into the
same holes as the top or bottom of the row before,
so that you do not leave a space between the rows.

To give the basket more definition, work the
outline in backstitch, with one strand of darkest
brown cotton in the needle.

The shades chosen would fit very well in a bed-
room colour scheme, but the sampler would look
equally attractive if the colours were changed for
stronger shades of green for the leaves and perhaps
red and dark magenta for the roses.

MAKING UP

Gently steam press the work on the wrong side and
mount it as explained on page 6. When framing the
picture, consider using a double mount with the
darker of the shades on the inside, to give your
sampler extra depth. Do not prepare your embroidery by lacing it over the mounting cardboard until
you have chosen your frame and decided whether
you will also require a mount (double or single).
These decisions will all affect the amount of fabric
that you will wish to leave around the edges of the
embroidered area.

ROSE SAMPLER ◄	DMC	ANCHOR	MADEIRA
╱ Light pink	3689	66	0606
: Medium pink	3688	68	0605
‹ Dark pink	3685	70	0514
› Light mauve	211	342	0801
╲ Medium mauve	210	109	0803
c̄ Dark mauve	208	111	0804
v Yellow	3078	292	0102
‡ Light blue	932	920	0907
+ Dark blue	311	148	1007
o Light green	369	213	1309
r Medium green	320	215	1311
s Dark green	319	217	1313
w Light brown	842	376	1910
x Medium brown	841	378	1911
z Dark brown	840	379	1912
Darkest brown*	938	381	2005

Darkest brown used for bks outline of basket only.

Pansies and Roses

This delightful placemat and napkin will certainly enhance any table setting, whether for a candlelit dinner or a summer party. You might vary the shades of the roses and pansies to match either your table setting, or perhaps the flowers from your own garden. If you want to change the design to make up an alternative set, you could quite easily adapt the motif to fit a corner instead of running down the side.

PANSIES AND ROSES

YOU WILL NEED

For one placemat, measuring 33cm × 47cm (13in × 19in), and one napkin, measuring 40cm (16in) square:

Ready-prepared placemat and napkin (for suppliers, see page 48), 26 threads to 2.5cm (1in)
Stranded embroidery cotton in the colours given in the panel
No24 tapestry needle

NOTE If you prefer not to use ready-prepared table linen, buy fabric with the same thread count. Work the embroidery first; trim to the correct size (including fringe), and withdraw a thread 12mm (½in) in from each edge. Neatly overcast every alternate thread, and then remove all cross threads below the stitched line to complete the fringe.

PREPARING THE FABRIC

First mark the centre (horizontal) line along the length of the placemat with a line of basting stitches. Measure in 2.5cm (1in) from the start of the fringe on the right-hand side and make a vertical line of basting stitches. Position the centre of the motif on the horizontal line of basting stitches and the right-hand edge of the motif along the vertical line of basting stitches. For the napkin, measure in and baste lines 12mm (½in) in from the edge, at one corner, as base lines for positioning.

Stretch the placemat or napkin in a frame (see page 5).

THE EMBROIDERY

Start at the centre of the appropriate motif and, using two strands of embroidery cotton in the needle, work each stitch over two threads of fabric in each direction. Make sure that all the top crosses run in the same direction and that each row is worked into the same holes as the top or bottom of the preceding row, so that you do not leave a space between rows.

Gently steam press the finished work on the wrong side to remove all creases.

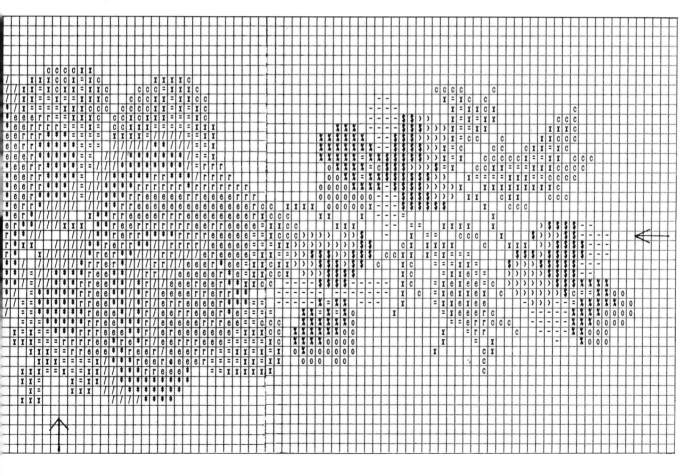

PANSIES AND ROSES		DMC	ANCHOR	MADEIRA
‡	Light pink	3609	85	0710
∕	Medium pink	3608	86	0709
r	Dark pink	718	88	0707
e	Darkest pink	915	89	0705
−	Light mauve	210	108	0803
⟩	Medium mauve	208	111	0804
$	Dark mauve	562	210	1202
%	Light yellow	3078	292	0102
o	Dark yellow	743	301	0113
c	Light green	3052	844	1509
x	Medium green	3347	266	1408
=	Dark green	3051	845	1508

Rose Cottage

Walk down the pathway of this
English cottage garden and take a
step back in time. In your
imagination, smell the sweet scent of
lavender and absorb the colours and
peacefulness of a bygone era.
The rambling roses around the cottage
door are embroidered with clusters of
french knots to give extra depth and
texture to this nostalgic design. It has
been set in a deep frame, but an
alternative idea would be to surround
it with a double mount, to add to the
sense of perspective.

ROSE COTTAGE

YOU WILL NEED

For the Rose Cottage, with a design area measuring 19.5cm × 15cm (7¾in × 6in), or 119 stitches by 85 stitches, here in a frame measuring 23cm × 18.5cm (9in × 7½in):

30cm × 25cm (12in × 10in) of Zweigart's white, 14-count Aida fabric
Stranded embroidery cotton in the colours given in the panel
No24 tapestry needle
Strong thread, for lacing across the back
Cardboard for mounting, sufficient to fit in the frame recess
Frame and mount of your choice

●

THE EMBROIDERY

Prepare the piece of fabric and stretch it in a frame as explained on page 5. Following the chart, start the embroidery at the centre of the design, using two strands of embroidery cotton in the needle. Work each stitch over a block of fabric in each direction. Make sure that all the top crosses run in the same direction and each row is worked into the same holes as the top or bottom of the row before, so that you do not leave a space between the rows.

Using backstitch, work all the outlines and markings with one strand of dark green cotton. Work the roses in clusters of medium and dark coloured pink french knots, using six strands of cotton in the needle and winding the cotton around the needle either once or twice, varying this so that some clusters of roses stand out more than others, to create a three-dimensional effect.

MAKING UP

Steam press the work on the wrong side and mount it as explained on page 6. Choose a mount and frame that are in keeping with the 'Olde Worlde' charm of the picture.

ROSE COTTAGE		DMC	ANCHOR	MADEIRA			DMC	ANCHOR	MADEIRA
∕	Light pink	776	73	0606	c	Cream	746	275	0101
:	Medium pink	894	26	0408	+	Light gold	676	887	2208
<	Dark pink	891	29	0412	n	Medium gold	729	890	2209
\	Light mauve	210	108	0803	g	Dark gold	680	901	2210
>	Medium mauve	208	111	0804	v	Yellow	743	301	0113
%	Dark mauve	550	101	0714	‡	Light blue	799	130	0910

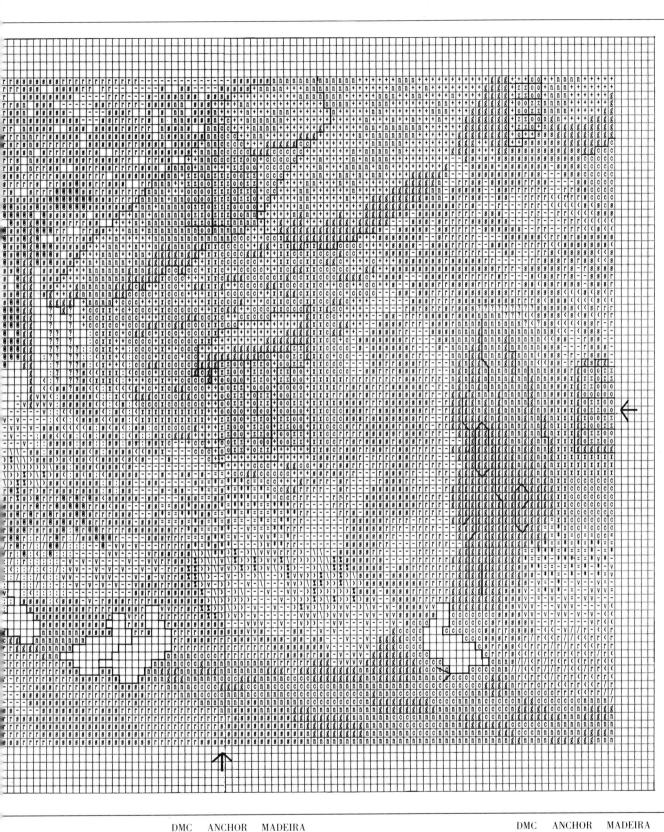

		DMC	ANCHOR	MADEIRA
=	Dark blue	798	131	0911
−	Light green	3348	264	1409
Г	Medium green	3347	266	1408
s	Dark green	3345	268	1406
@	Darkest green	936	263	1507
x	Light brown	434	365	2009

		DMC	ANCHOR	MADEIRA
?	Dark brown	829	906	2106
o	Light grey	762	234	1804
z	Dark grey	414	399	1801

Baskets and Wreaths

A profusion of white lace and flowers gives a light and airy feel to these cushions. The bright shades of the roses are complemented by the gentler blue and mauve flowers, making this trio a delightful addition to any home.

BASKETS AND WREATHS

YOU WILL NEED

For each cushion, measuring 40cm (16in) square:

*21.5cm (8½in) square of Zweigart's white,
14-count Aida fabric
Stranded embroidery cotton in the colours given
in the panel
No24 tapestry needle
42cm (16½in) square of lace fabric
Two 42cm (16½in) squares of white backing fabric
85cm (34in) of gathered lace edging, 5cm (2in)
wide, for the edge of the embroidered panel
1.8m (2yds) of gathered lace edging, 4cm (1½in)
wide, for the edge of the cushion
42.5cm (17in) square cushion pad*

*NOTE If you are making the easy care cover, you
will require, in place of the two squares of backing
fabric, one 42cm (16½in) square and two more
pieces, both 42cm (16½in) long, one 23cm (9in)
wide, and one 33cm (13in) wide*

•

THE EMBROIDERY

Prepare the fabric and stretch it in a frame as explained on page 5. Following the chart, start the embroidery at the centre of the design, using two strands of embroidery cotton in the needle. Work each stitch over a block of fabric in each direction, making sure that all the top crosses run in the same direction and each row is worked into the same holes as the top or bottom of the row before, so that you do not leave a space between the rows.

MAKING UP

Each cover is made up in the same way. Gently steam press the embroidered fabric on the wrong side, then turn under 12mm (½in) on all sides, mitring the corners as explained on page 6. Baste the wider of the lace edgings around the embroidered fabric, positioning it just under the turned edge and joining the ends of the lace together with a narrow french seam.

Centre the panel over the lace fabric. Pin it in position and then appliqué the panel to the lace by slipstitching around the edge through all layers. Take the remaining lace edging and, again joining the ends with a narrow french seam, pin and baste it

around the edge of the lace fabric. The decorative edge should face inward and the straight edge of the lace should lie parallel to the edge of the fabric and just inside the 12mm (½in) seam allowance.

Take one of the pieces of backing fabric and lay the prepared lace fabric over it, still with the frill lying flat on the lace, facing inward. With the wrong side of the lace fabric to the right side of the backing, pin, baste and stitch through all three layers, stitching through the straight edge of the lace, just within the 12mm (½in) seam allowance.

With right sides together, join the remaining piece of backing fabric to the cushion front, leaving a 25cm (10in) gap at one side. Turn the cover right side out; insert the cushion pad, and slipstitch to close.

EASY CARE VERSION

If you prefer a cover that can quickly be slipped off and on, for ease of laundering, you can make one with an overlap across the centre back.

Make up the front of the cover as described above. Take the wider of the two pieces of backing fabric; neaten one of the long edges and then press and stitch a 12mm (½in) hem. Take the other piece, and again on a long edge turn under 6mm (¼in) and then a further 12mm (½in) and hem. Lay the shorter piece over the longer one, overlapping the prepared edges, to make a 42cm (16½in) square; baste and stitch the sides.

Place the prepared back and cushion front with right sides together and, taking a 12mm (½in) seam, stitch all around the edge. Turn the cover right side out and insert the cushion pad through the opening across the back.

BASKETS AND WREATHS ▶	DMC	ANCHOR	MADEIRA
< Light pink	776	73	0606
+ Medium pink	894	26	0408
o Dark pink	892	28	0413
@ Mauve	208	111	0804
v Yellow	745	292	0112
% Light blue	932	920	1602
− Dark blue	930	922	1005
s Light green	369	213	1309
= Medium green	368	214	1310
‡ Dark green	367	216	1312
x Light brown	950	882	2309
> Dark brown	407	914	2312

Note: the same combination is used for the Baskets design and the Wreaths design, on pages 30-31.

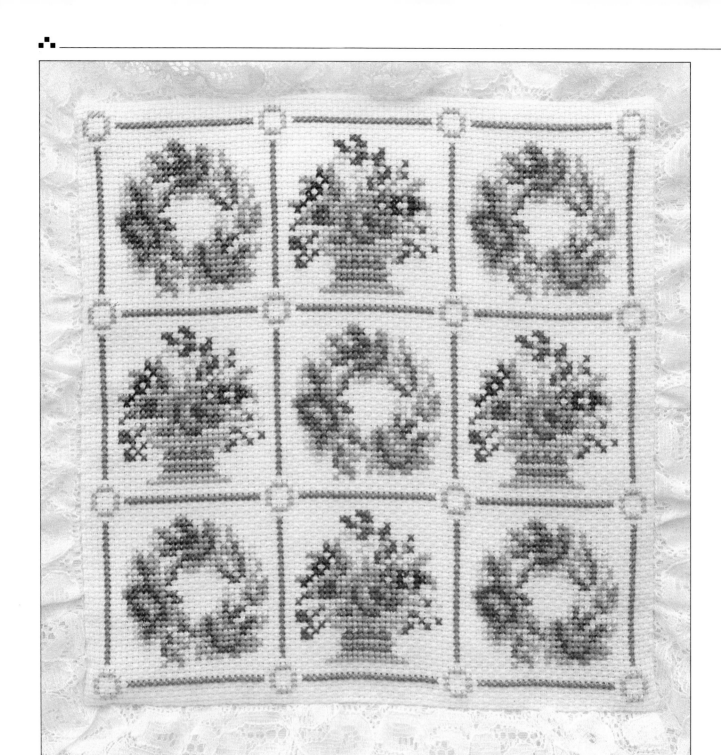

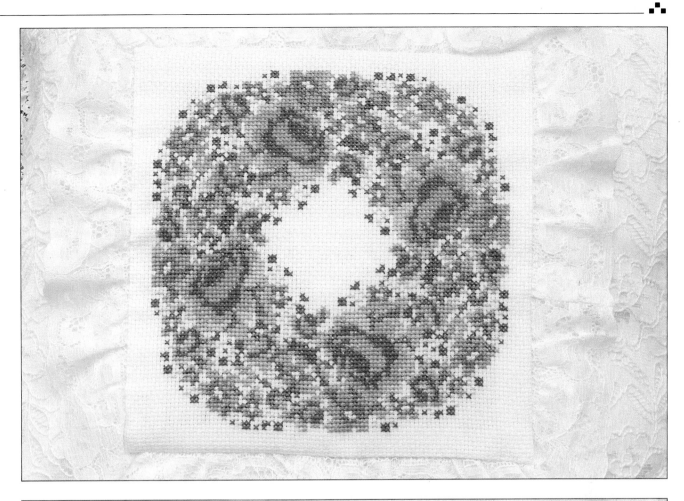

29

Basket cushion ▲

Wreath cushion ▶

BASKET CUSHION AND WREATH CUSHION

		DMC	ANCHOR	MADEIRA			DMC	ANCHOR	MADEIRA
−	Light pink	776	73	0606	=	Dark blue	930	922	1005
:	Medium pink	894	26	0408	<	Light green	369	213	1309
o	Dark pink	892	28	0413	%	Medium green	368	214	1310
x	Mauve	208	111	0804	‡	Dark green	367	216	1312
v	Yellow	745	292	0112	c	Light brown	950	882	2309
/	Light blue	932	920	1602	+	Dark brown	407	914	2312

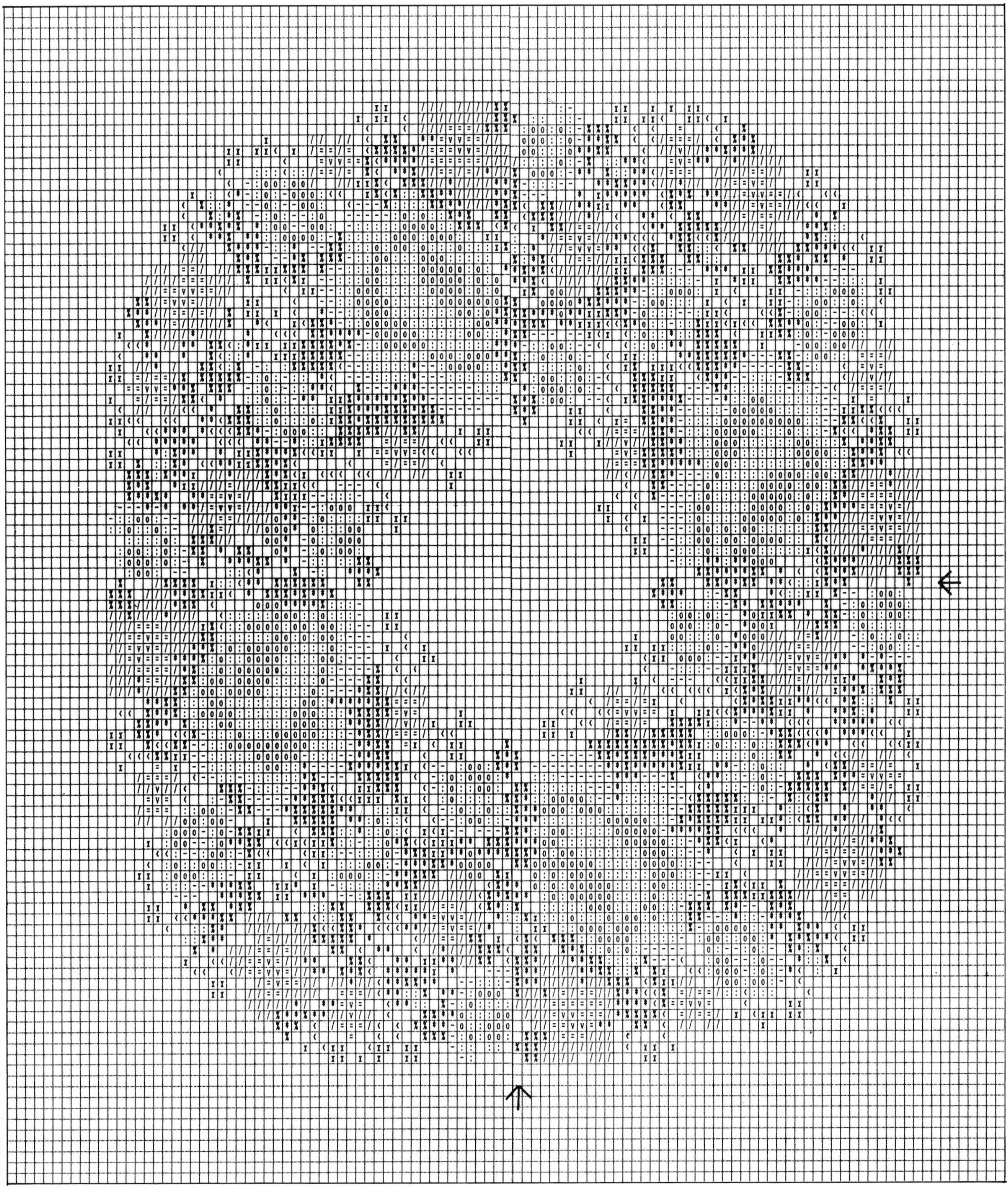

Summer Picture

This bouquet of peach and pink roses is just as fresh as the moment it was picked on a balmy summer's day. The subtle shades of the roses make this picture an ideal focal point for anyone fond of pastel shades. Alternatively, you might choose to embroider the roses in shades of dark pink and red to give warmth and vibrance to the design.

The design has been shown here as a picture, but you could, of course, make it into a cushion cover, similar to those on the preceding pages.

SUMMER PICTURE

YOU WILL NEED

For the Summer picture, with a design area measuring 19cm (7½in) square, or 110 stitches by 108 stitches, here in a frame measuring 36cm (14½in) square:

29cm (11½in) of Zweigart's white, 14-count Aida fabric
Stranded embroidery cotton in the colours given in the panel
No24 tapestry needle
Strong thread, for lacing across the back
Cardboard, for mounting, sufficient to fit into the frame recess
Frame and mount of your choice

•

THE EMBROIDERY

Prepare the fabric and stretch it in a frame as explained on page 5. Following the chart, start the embroidery at the centre of the design, using two strands of embroidery cotton in the needle. Work each stitch over one block of fabric in each direction. Make sure that all the top crosses run in the same direction and each row is worked into the same holes as the top or bottom of the row before, so that you do not leave a space between the rows.

MAKING UP

Gently steam press the work on the wrong side and mount it as explained on page 6. Choose a mount and frame to match your colour scheme.

SUMMER PICTURE ▶	DMC	ANCHOR	MADEIRA
‡ Light pink	3689	66	0606
⁄ Medium pink	3688	68	0605
r Dark pink	3687	69	0604
e Darkest pink	3685	70	0514
% Light peach	948	778	0306
a Medium peach	754	868	0305
o Dark peach	353	6	0304
n Darkest peach	352	9	0303
c Light green	3348	264	1409
x Medium green	3347	266	1408
= Dark green	937	268	1504
s Light brown	950	882	2309
@ Dark brown	407	914	2312

Greetings Cards

Whichever of these attractive greetings cards you embroider, the result will provide a lasting reminder of a special occasion, as the finished card can easily be framed.

GREETINGS CARDS

YOU WILL NEED

For either the Rosy Posy card or the Wild Rose card, each measuring 15cm × 20.5cm (6in × 8in) overall, with a portrait cut-out measuring 11cm × 15cm (4½in × 6in):

15cm × 19cm (6in × 7½in) of Zweigart's cream, 18-count Aida fabric
Stranded embroidery cotton in the colours given in the appropriate panel
No24 tapestry needle
Card mount, landscape or portrait, as required (for suppliers, see page 48)

For the Rose Garland card, measuring 15.5cm × 11cm (6¼in × 4½in), with a cut-out measuring 8cm (3in) in diameter:

10cm (4in) square of Zweigart's cream, 18-count Aida fabric
Stranded embroidery cotton in the colours given in the appropriate panel
No24 tapestry needle
Card mount (for suppliers, see page 48)

•

THE EMBROIDERY

Prepare the fabric for your chosen card and stretch it in a frame as explained on page 5. Following the appropriate chart, start the embroidery at the centre of the design, using one strand of embroidery cotton in the needle. Work each stitch over one block of fabric in each direction. Make sure that all the top crosses go in the same direction and that each row is worked into the same holes as the top or bottom of the row before, so that you do not leave a space between the rows.

MAKING UP THE CARDS

Trim the embroidery to about 12mm (½in) larger than the cut-out window. Open out the self-adhesive mount and centre your embroidery behind the aperture. Fold the card and press firmly to secure. Some cards require a dab of glue for a secure and neat finish.

WILD ROSE ▶		DMC	ANCHOR	MADEIRA
⊡	Light pink	818	48	0502
△	Medium pink	776	73	0606
⊟	Dark pink	899	40	0609
⊞	Light yellow	3078	292	0102
+	Medium yellow	743	301	0113
⊹	Light green	3348	264	1409
⊞	Medium green	3347	266	1408
◆	Dark green	3345	268	1406
⊡	Light brown	434	365	2009
●	Medium brown	829	906	2106

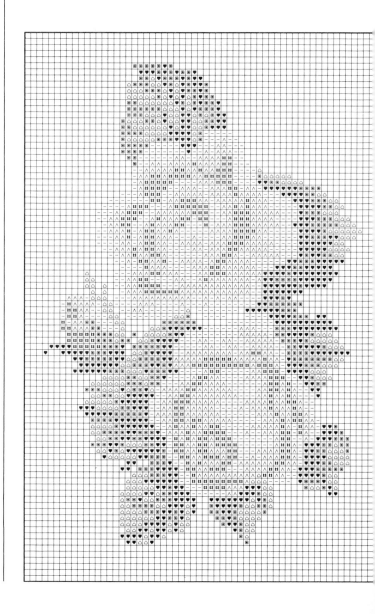

ROSY POSY ◄		DMC	ANCHOR	MADEIRA
⊟	Light pink	894	26	0408
∧	Medium pink	892	28	0413
⊞	Dark pink	304	47	0511
⌂	Light green	3348	264	1409
⊡	Medium green	3052	844	1509
♥	Dark green	3051	845	1508

ROSE GARLAND ▶		DMC	ANCHOR	MADEIRA
◿	Light pink	776	73	0606
⋈	Medium pink	899	40	0609
▲	Dark pink	309	42	0510
⊥	Light peach	948	778	0306
⊞	Medium peach	353	6	0304
▨	Dark peach	754	868	0305
⊠	Yellow	743	301	0113
�	Light blue	932	920	1602
▬	Medium blue	931	921	1003
♥	Dark blue	930	922	1005
▷	Light green	3348	264	1409
Ｍ	Medium green	470	266	1502
▼	Dark green	936	263	1507

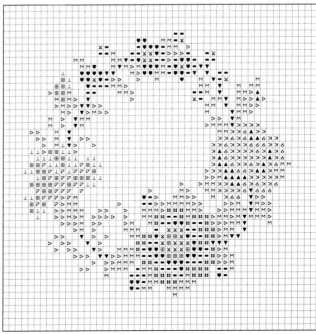

Botanical
Sampler

Look through a text book on roses
and, alongside the more familiar
names of your favourite species, you
will find their scientific names. In this
design, the Latin names have been
used as a frame for the beautiful
blooms of a selection of our more
traditional roses.
Set in a frame with an appropriate
period air, this beautiful sampler
will make an attractive focal point
in any room.

BOTANICAL SAMPLER

For the sampler, with a design area measuring 17cm × 23.5cm (6¾in × 9½in), or 103 stitches by 133 stitches, here in a frame measuring 27.5cm × 33cm (11in × 13in):

27cm × 33.5cm (10¾in × 13¼in) of Zweigart's cream, 14-count Aida fabric
Stranded embroidery cotton in the colours given in the panel
No24 tapestry needle
Strong thread, for lacing across the back
Cardboard, for mounting, sufficient to fit into the frame recess
Frame of your choice

•

THE EMBROIDERY

Prepare the fabric and stretch it in a frame as explained on page 5. Following the chart, start the embroidery at the centre of the design, using two strands of embroidery cotton in the needle. Work each stitch over one block of fabric in each direction. Make sure that all the top crosses run in the same direction and that each row is worked into the same holes as the top or bottom of the row before, leaving no spaces between the rows.

Make french knots for seeds in the bottom left-hand corner with six and three strands of light and medium green stranded cotton respectively, winding the cotton once around the needle and using the picture as a guide. Make the straight lines in back-stitch with three strands of light green cotton.

Work the names around the outside in backstitch using two strands of dark brown cotton, and the branches with two strands of medium brown cotton.

MAKING UP

Gently steam press the work on the wrong side and mount as explained on page 6. Set your finished sampler in a traditional frame.

BOTANICAL SAMPLER ▶		DMC	ANCHOR	MADEIRA
‡	Light pink	605	50	0613
∕	Medium pink	604	60	0614
r	Dark pink	603	62	0701
e	Darkest pink	602	63	0702
−	Light mauve	210	108	0803
〉	Medium mauve	208	111	0804
$	Dark mauve	550	101	0714
%	Light yellow	3078	292	0102
a	Medium yellow	743	301	0113
o	Dark yellow	742	302	0107
c	Light green	3348	264	1409
x	Medium green	3347	266	1408
=	Dark green	937	268	1504
s	Light brown	640	393	1905
\	Medium brown	841	378	1911
	Dark brown*	938	381	2005

* Used for bks writing.

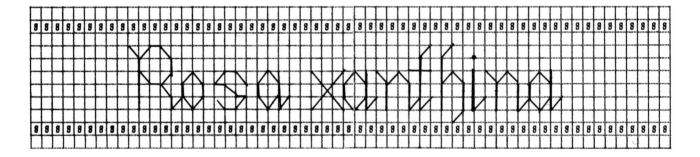

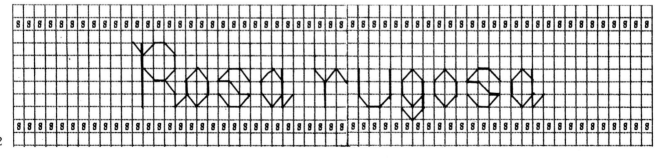

Rosa xanthina

Rosa rugosa

Small Gifts

A peach rose on the pincushion is
edged with a delicate cream border,
echoed by broderie anglaise.
The bag, filled with lavender from your
garden, will remind you of summer
throughout the rest of the year.
To complete the trio, there is a
bookmark with a lacy trim.

SMALL GIFTS

YOU WILL NEED

For the pincushion, measuring 17.5cm (7in) square, excluding the lace:

25cm (10in) square of Zweigart's cream, 14-count Aida fabric
20cm (8in) square of cream backing fabric
1.6m (1¾yds) of cream broderie anglaise, 5cm (2in) wide
4 pale peach ribbon roses
Stranded embroidery cotton in the colours given in the panel
No24 tapestry needle
Polyester filling

For the lavender bag, measuring 12.5cm × 17cm (5in × 6¾in):

20cm × 22cm (8in × 8½in) of Zweigart's cream, 14-count Aida fabric
15cm × 17cm (6in × 6½in) of cream backing fabric
35cm (14in) of cream broderie anglaise, 5cm (2in) wide
50cm (20in) of peach satin ribbon, 6mm (¼in) wide
Stranded embroidery cotton in the colours given in the panel
No24 tapestry needle

For the bookmark, measuring 9cm × 20.5cm (3½in × 8in):

Stranded embroidery cotton in the colours given in the panel
No24 tapestry needle
Prepared bookmark, in ivory (for suppliers, see page 48)

•

THE EMBROIDERY

Stretch the fabric for the pincushion or the lavender bag in a hoop or frame, as explained on page 5. The bookmark may be held in the hand when working the embroidery.

Following the correct chart, start the embroidery at the centre of the design, using two strands of embroidery cotton in the needle for the pincushion or lavender bag and one strand for the bookmark. Work each stitch over one block of fabric in each

direction. Make sure that all the top crosses run in the same direction and that each row is worked into the same holes as the top or bottom of the row before, so that you do not leave a space between rows. Lightly steam press the finished embroidery.

MAKING THE PINCUSHION

Trim the embroidery to measure 20cm (8in) square. Using a tiny french seam, join the short edges of the broderie anglaise together, then run a gathering thread close to the straight edge of the lace. Pulling up the gathers to fit, lay the lace on the right side of the embroidery, with the decorative edge facing inward and the straight edge parallel to the edge of the fabric and just inside the 12mm (½in) seam allowance. Baste in position, adjusting the gathers to allow extra fullness at the corners. Machine in place.

With right sides together, pin and machine the backing fabric and the embroidered piece together, enclosing the broderie anglaise edging and leaving a gap of 5cm (2in) at one side. Trim across the corners; turn the pincushion right side out, and insert the polyester filling. Slipstitch the opening to close it.

Lavender bag ▼

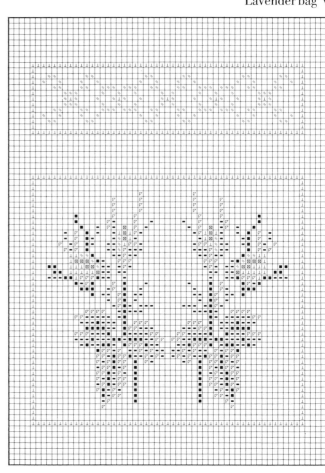

MAKING THE LAVENDER BAG

Trim the embroidered fabric to measure 15cm × 17cm (6in × 6½in). With right sides together, baste and machine stitch the embroidery to the backing fabric, stitching down the sides and across the bottom and taking a 12mm (½in) seam allowance.

Turn to the right side. Turn a single 12mm (½in) hem around the top. Join the short edges of the broderie anglaise with a tiny french seam, then run a gathering thread close to the straight edge of the lace. Pulling up the gathers to fit and with the right side of the lace to the wrong side of the bag, baste and then machine stitch the broderie anglaise in place around the top of the bag. Gently steam press.

Fill the bag with lavender and tie with a ribbon, placing it around the space between the two areas of embroidery.

BOOKMARK, LAVENDER BAG AND PINCUSHION ▼		DMC	ANCHOR	MADEIRA
◻	Cream	746	275	0101
⊥	Light peach	353	6	0304
⊠	Dark peach	352	9	0303
☑	Light green	3348	264	1409
▬	Medium green	3052	844	1509
■	Dark green*	936	263	1507

* Dark green used for bks outline of roses on pincushion only.

Bookmark ▼

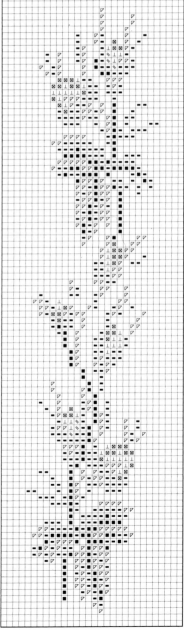

Pincushion ▼

ACKNOWLEDGEMENTS

The author would like to thank the following people for their help with projects in this book:

Kate Riley, Jenny Thorpe, Lyn Freeman, Cilla King, Diane Teal and especially Helen Burke.

Thanks are also due to DMC Creative World Ltd, for supplying fabrics and threads, Mike Grey at Framecraft Miniatures Limited for the table linen, box and picture frame, and the staff of Speedframe at 140 High Street, Lincoln, for their excellent framing service.

Embroidery kits designed by Jane Alford may be obtained from her company:

Reflexions,
The Stables,
Black Bull Yard,
Welton,
Lincoln LN2 3HZ

SUPPLIERS

The following mail order company has supplied some of the basic items needed for making up the projects in this book:

Framecraft Miniatures Limited
148-150 High Street
Aston
Birmingham, B6 4US
England
Telephone (021) 359 4442

Addresses for Framecraft stockists worldwide
Ireland Needlecraft Pty. Ltd.
2-4 Keppel Drive
Hallam, Victoria 3803
Australia

Danish Art Needlework
PO Box 442, Lethbridge
Alberta T1J 3Z1
Canada

Sanyei Imports
PO Box 5, Hashima Shi
Gifu 501-62
Japan

The Embroidery Shop
286 Queen Street
Masterton
New Zealand

Anne Brinkley Designs Inc.
246 Walnut Street
Newton
Mass. 02160
USA

S A Threads and Cottons Ltd.
43 Somerset Road
Cape Town
South Africa

For information on your nearest stockist of embroidery cotton, contact the following:

DMC

UK
DMC Creative World Limited
62 Pullman Road
Wigston
Leicester, LE8 2DY
Telephone: 0533 811040

USA
The DMC Corporation
Port Kearney Bld.
10 South Kearney
N.J. 07032-0650
Telephone: 201 589 0606

AUSTRALIA
DMC Needlecraft Pty
P.O. Box 317
Earlswood 2206
NSW 2204
Telephone: 02599 3088

COATS AND ANCHOR

UK
Kilncraigs Mill
Alloa
Clackmannanshire
Scotland, FK10 1EG
Telephone: 0259 723431

USA
Coats & Clark
P.O. Box 27067
Dept CO1
Greenville
SC 29616
Telephone: 803 234 0103

AUSTRALIA
Coats Patons Crafts
Thistle Street
Launceston
Tasmania 7250
Telephone: 00344 4222

MADEIRA

UK
Madeira Threads (UK) Limited
Thirsk Industrial Park
York Road, Thirsk
N. Yorkshire, YO7 3BX
Telephone: 0845 524880

U.S.A.
Madeira Marketing Limited
600 East 9th Street
Michigan City
IN 46360
Telephone: 219 873 1000

AUSTRALIA
Penguin Threads Pty Limited
25-27 Izett Street
Prahran
Victoria 3181
Telephone: 03529 4400